The Slavs and the Slave Trade: The History of Enslaved Slavs across Eastern Europe and the Islamic World

By Charles River Editors

About Charles River Editors

Charles River Editors provides superior editing and original writing services across the digital publishing industry, with the expertise to create digital content for publishers across a vast range of subject matter. In addition to providing original digital content for third party publishers, we also republish civilization's greatest literary works, bringing them to new generations of readers via ebooks.

Sign up here to receive updates about free books as we publish them, and visit Our Kindle Author Page to browse today's free promotions and our most recently published Kindle titles.

Introduction

It has often been said that the greatest invention of all time was the sail, which facilitated the internationalization of the globe and thus ushered in the modern era. Columbus' contact with the New World, alongside European maritime contact with the Far East, transformed human history, and in particular the history of Africa.

It was the sail that linked the continents of Africa and America, and thus it was also the sail that facilitated the greatest involuntary human migration of all time. The African slave trade is a complex and deeply divisive subject that has had a tendency to evolve according the political requirements of any given age, and is often touchable only with the correct distribution of culpability. It has for many years, therefore, been deemed singularly unpalatable to implicate Africans themselves in the perpetration of the institution, and only in recent years has the large-scale African involvement in both the Atlantic and Indian Ocean Slave Trades come to be an accepted fact. There can, however, be no doubt that even though large numbers of indigenous Africans were liable, it was European ingenuity and greed that fundamentally drove the industrialization of the Transatlantic slave trade in response to massive new market demands created by their equally ruthless exploitation of the Americas.

The East African Slave Trade on the other hand, or the Indian Ocean Slave Trade as it was also known, was a far more complex and nuanced phenomenon, far older, significantly more widespread, rooted in ancient traditions, and governed by rules very different to those in the western hemisphere. It is also often referred to as the Arab Slave Trade, although this, specifically, might perhaps be more accurately applied to the more ancient variant of organized African slavery, affecting North Africa, and undertaken prior to the advent of Islam and certainly prior to the spread of the institution south as far as the south/east African coast. It also involved the slavery of non-African races and was, therefore, more general in scope.

Islamic slave traders engaged in a particular form of ethnically-based slavery. Whereas for much of human history slavery was somewhat arbitrary, in its later forms it often had a discriminatory component, typically based on race, ethnicity, nationality or religion. This distinction shows how the practitioners of slavery justified the practice in terms of ideology, and Slavic people were discriminated against within the Ottoman Empire. Slavs had lived in the lands of today's Eastern European region for centuries. Slavic peoples were essentially native of Eurasia and settled in the Black Sea region and other parts of today's Balkans, Eastern Europe, the Caucasus and Central Asia. One of their first major political representatives, however, was the *Rus*, which founded a settlement near today's Kiev in Ukraine from the 9th century. The Kievan Rus was a major regional power until its demise in the thirteenth century after which the mantle of the *Rus* was eventually taken up by the Grand Duchy of Moscow. The lands making up modern-day Ukraine were contested for much of the following centuries and were the base for a key section of the slave trade. The *Rus* were recorded trading slaves on the Volga route, from today's northwestern Russia in the ninth century, with the Muslim world via the Volga River and the Caspian Sea, as well as a separate route via the Dnieper River. Accounts from this period show the use of slaves by the *Rus* as well as involvement in the slave trade itself. For instance, Ibn Faḍlān's writing from the early tenth century from Baghdad, concerning talks with the King of the Volga Bulghars, has been cited by historians as crucial in understanding the Middle East and Slavic regions during this era.[1] Ibn Faḍlān wrote about the importance of slaves in the Rus world.[2]

Indeed, some historians have aligned the term Slav as deriving from descriptions of slaves: "The word "slave" and its cognates in most modern European languages is itself derived from "sclavus," meaning "slav," the ethnic name for the inhabitants of this region."[3] Some historians have outlined how they believe that Slavic slaves were used intensively in the ninth and tenth centuries and acted as a driver of Western European economic growth and allowed them to "emerge from the Dark Ages." It is only fair to note that this assertion has been disputed. Separately, other scholars have asserted that Constantinople's rapid rise to become one of Europe's largest cities was fueled by a large supply of Slavic slaves.[4]

These trans-European routes diminished somewhat from the thirteenth century but demonstrated how common slave trading was in the region during these centuries. The majority of the people would have been kidnapped from Southeast Europe, as well as the Eurasian and Caucasus regions. Today, that encompasses Russia, Ukraine, Georgia, the Baltic states, Poland, Romania, Bulgaria, and the states of the former Yugoslavia. Crucially, an important component of Slavic identity was the Christian faith, in particular Orthodox Christianity.

In the medieval period, a slave trading network became more entrenched, transporting people from Slavic lands in Eastern Europe to the Mediterranean and beyond. The growing schism between the Catholic and Orthodox versions of Christianity made Orthodox Christians targets of the former's slave traders. As a result, Slavic slaves were captured and taken to parts of Christian Spain, including Aragon and Valencia, in the fourteenth and fifteenth centuries.[5]

Many of the slaves would be put to work in the expanding Islamic world. The term *Saqaliba* was used in Arabic to denote slaves of central and Eastern European origin, but over time the term became more generally attached to European slaves more broadly. As well as the Volga

---

[1] James E. Montgomery, Ibn Faḍlān and the Rusiyyah, *Journal of Arabic and Islamic Studies*, 3, (2000) 1–25.
[2] Ibid.
[3] Citing Duncan Clarke's *Slaves and Slavery* (1998), in: George Pavlu, "Recalling Africa's harrowing tale of its first slavers – The Arabs – as UK Slave Trade Abolition is commemorated," *New African*, 27 March 2018, https://newafricanmagazine.com/16616/, [Accessed 23 June 2021]
[4] Marek Jankowiak, Dirhams for slaves: Investigating the Slavic slave trade in the tenth century, Medievalists (2012) https://www.medievalists.net/2016/02/dirhams-for-slaves-investigating-the-slavic-slave-trade-in-the-tenth-century/, [Accessed 17 June 2021]
[5] Johan MacKechnie, "Justifying Slavery", *History Today* (67:5, May 2017), https://www.historytoday.com/justifying-slavery, [Accessed 22 June 2021]

route, Slavic slaves would be traded through the Balkans as well as through continental Europe to Spain and North Africa. Muslim rule in Spain spanned, to some extent, from around the eighth century to the mid-sixteenth century. The Spanish Caliphate, in particular, used Slavic slaves for military purposes, offering the hope of some degree of freedom with advancement through the ranks, and eunuchs were also widely used in Spain. As male slaves who were castrated, eunuchs had a long-standing role in many countries for centuries, and it was common for slaves to be castrated upon or before arrival in Muslim territory. As well as military recruits and eunuchs, *Saqaliba* also involved the use of slaves in a harem of concubines as well as servants. A number of these roles would continue for centuries and into the modern era, most notably in the Ottoman Empire.

The Slavs and the Slave Trade: The History of Enslaved Slavs across Europe and the Islamic World

About Charles River Editors

Introduction

    The Ottoman Empire

    Crimea and the Black Sea

    The Cossacks and Russia

    The Decline of the Slave Trade in Eastern Europe

    Online Resources

    Further Reading

Free Books by Charles River Editors

Discounted Books by Charles River Editors

The Ottoman Empire

The Ottoman Empire is perhaps one of history's most enigmatic dynasties. In power from the late thirteenth century until the beginning of the twentieth century, the Ottoman Empire dominated the Middle East, North Africa and much of South East Europe for most of this period. The Ottomans also gained territory in the Caucasus and parts of the Black Sea region. Seeing themselves as the protectors of the Islamic faith, the Ottomans had somewhat of a unifying impact; nevertheless, when Ottoman armies came into contact with non-Muslim populations and lands, it presented challenges for the imperial rulers.

A number of structural elements made the Ottoman Empire unique and proved important in the persistence of the slave trade into the empire. First, the empire was relatively tolerant of different faiths, marking it out as different from its contemporaries in Europe. Nevertheless, this did not translate to equality between faiths, merely that Islam was the most important religion in the empire and others were tolerated. Legally, this meant that trading slaves was relatively unproblematic. Second, the early centuries of Ottoman rule led to huge territorial gains and a fearsome reputation on the battlefield. A key victory in the growth of Ottoman prestige was its capture of Constantinople (today's Istanbul) from the Orthodox Christian Byzantine Empire in 1453. Suleiman the Magnificent, in particular, who ruled from 1520 until 1566, expanded the empire's lands and famously reached Vienna, before being repelled by other European powers. At its peak the Ottoman Empire revolved around Constantinople as its central point, with trade taking place within the empire, with aligned states and territories, as well as outside powers. While not as sophisticated as later capitalist trading networks, the Ottomans nevertheless exploited trade contacts to become one of the world's most developed and wealthiest regions. However, having acquired vast swathes of territory in Africa, Asia and Europe, the Ottomans went into slow decline right up until the twentieth century. As a result, the perennial weakness of the Ottomans meant much of its land was contested in the final centuries of its existence.

The slave trade prospered with the Ottoman Empire partly through the patchwork of states and disintegrated empires of the past. Most notably, this involved the khanates, such as in Crimea, that were located deep into a nominally Slavic region. These outposts exploited surrounding areas as a source of slave labor and were often the "spoils" of war or a form of currency or reparations. This study will mainly, although not exclusively, focus on this trade of Slavic slaves into the Ottoman Empire.

As a separate element of historical context, it is worth briefly setting out the legacy of the Mongol Empire in Eurasia. The remnants of the Mongol Empire played a key part in the Slavic slave trade. It should also be pointed out that the Mongols traded slaves with the Byzantine Empire and therefore preceded the specifically Slavic trade with the Ottomans.[6] The Mongol

---

[6] Bayarsaikhan Dashdondog (2019). The Black Sea Slave Trade in the 13th–14th century That Changed the Political Balance in the Near East. *Golden Horde Review*. 7. 283-294.

Empire, also known as the Golden Horde, mainly converted to Islam during the thirteenth century and in the course of the next century, the empire itself would recede and finally vanish, at the same time as the Ottomans were growing their power in the Middle East. What was left of the Mongol Empire in Eurasia were small outposts that resisted the rising regional, and Christian, powers. This meant that other states, such as Lithuania, Poland, Russia and the Cossack Hetmanate republic would all try to dominate, go to war and often find accommodation with these historical remnants.

One of the persistent themes of Slavic slavery was its connection with war reparations, or put more simply, as the "spoils of war." The Crimean Khanate, and the Ottomans more broadly, removed adults and children from conquered populations as a levy as well as a more insidious form of control. A clear example of this was the Ottoman practice of *devshirme*. The Ottomans are thought to started *devshirme* soon after they built an empire and certainly it was in full force by the mid-fifteenth century. The system was sometimes considered a "blood tax" on families in the Balkans and Anatolian regions and is thought to have impacted between half a million and one million children and adolescents.

Devshirme involved removing Christian children aged between 8 and 18 years old from families in the Balkans, a region the Ottomans dominated until the nineteenth century. The children were then forcibly converted to Islam and trained as administrators and soldiers. Indeed, *devshirme* produced many grand viziers, a position effectively second in command of the entire empire after the sultan. For the military track, *devshirme* children were often enrolled in the janissaries, an elite core of soldiers. The janissaries were strictly trained and used as a distinct military unit, which became a formidable force. The janissaries could be more clearly seen as slaves than the administrator track, but nevertheless they also received payment. As the Ottoman Empire progressed, the janissaries were so numerous they formed a cohesive political bloc and tried to exert influence over the Sultan and the wider empire.

The *devshirme* system was a particular Ottoman form of power. Removing children from families was clearly deeply resented and was a form of Christian slavery. Yet, these children could then also achieve advancement unthinkable for other Christians within the empire. Forced to convert to Islam, it also left no doubt to the hierarchy of religion under Ottoman rule. Instituting different classes of people within an empire was not novel, but was perhaps less draconian than its contemporaries; nevertheless, the practice was subsequently abolished despite protests from defenders of the system. The janissaries would have political clout into the nineteenth century, by which time the empire was beginning to fray.

The situation for Christians and Jews outside the Ottoman Empire but within striking distance of Tatar raids could be precarious. It was precisely these, as well as other groups, who were targets for raiders and slave traders. For Christians and Jews within the borders of the empire, however, living conditions were different. The faiths were viewed as forerunners, and part of the theological family, of Islam. As a result, Christians and Jews were known as *dhimmis* within the Ottoman Empire: second class citizens who had some freedoms and legal protections. As we have already seen, there was tolerance of other religions within the empire and other groups were allowed to practice their faith although this came with certain restrictions. There was a caveat, however, by which Christians and Jews had to pay separate taxes, known as *jizya*, a poll tax, and *kharaj*, a land tax.[7] *Dhimmis* were also required to maintain loyalty to the Muslim commonwealth or *Ummah*. The concept of the *dhimma* dates back centuries in the Islamic world. As historian Anh Nga Longva has written, the concept meant that "Muslim rulers [would] grant hospitality and protection to members of other revealed religions, on condition that the latter acknowledged the domination of Islam."[8] If someone protected under the *dhimmi* law broke the agreement—for instance by committing treason or rebellion or failing to pay taxes—and left the empire, they were then treated similarly to others outside Ottoman control: that is to say liable to be captured and enslaved. Not paying the requisite taxes could also land someone in prison. Nevertheless, keeping in mind the Ottoman Empire developed in the same way European states could still be described as medieval, rule under the Sultan was perhaps relatively enlightened: "The *dhimma* grants non-Muslims the public right to live in Muslim territories, and the private rights to buy, sell, and own; to marry, have children, and inherit; and to have access to courts of law."[9]

Taken together, the *dhimma* system granted significant rights to Jews and Christians within Ottoman territory. They were also exempt from conscription into the Ottoman army. These rights, even as second-class citizens, can be juxtaposed against the slaves captured outside the empire and traded within it, which displayed a much harsher, often cruel tenet. Slavery was justified in economic and practical terms, as well as geopolitics. As we have seen, the Ottomans predominantly took slaves as a form of control and as reward for military victories, while the slaves themselves had a variety of roles, fulfilling both highly-skilled and menial tasks. Some of the slaves came from Central Europe, such as from the Habsburg Empire, while others came from North Africa, from today's Tunisia and Algeria. The latter route was known as the Barbary slave trade. The Ottomans also had trading contacts, including with slaves, with the Italian city-states of Venice and Genoa. It has been documented how the Ottomans had an unofficial presence in Venice from the fourteenth and fifteenth centuries.[10] Italian city-states in the medieval period were themselves not only heavily involved in the slave trading, including to the Ottoman Empire but also the movement of Muslim slaves. Indeed, it provides context for the trade of Slavic slaves that the practice was common in many other states, and was far from regimented in terms of selecting certain religions or ethnicities. One article from 2018 focuses on

---

[7] Anh Nga Longva, "From the Dhimma to the capitulations: memory and experience of protection in Lebanon," *Religious Minorities in the Middle East: Domination, Self-Empowerment, Accommodation* (Brill, 2012), p. 49.
[8] Ibid.
[9] Ibid.
[10] Maria Pia Pedani, "Ottoman Merchants in the Adriatic. Trade and Smuggling," Acta Histriae, (16, 2008, 155-172), 159.

the development of Slavic slavery through Venice, mainly from today's Bosnia, stating, "The most important source of slaves in medieval Europe was the coast of Bosnia on the eastern shores of the Adriatic Sea. For various reasons, including the harshness of the terrain and endemic warfare among local clans, Bosnia proved the most convenient and long-lasting of these slave-supplying regions. From there, Slavs were shipped as slaves by Venetian merchants, to supply new markets in the Islamic world."[11]

Nevertheless, the Venetians and Ottomans eventually came to an agreement forbidding the use of slaves, although the situation was often in flux.[12] The majority of slaves to the Ottoman Empire, however, came along the Black Sea route and involved Slavic peoples. This will form the bulk of the rest of this book.

Crimea and the Black Sea

Historians have long identified the Black Sea region as crucial as a source of slaves. In fact, there is some evidence to suggest that the Roman and Byzantium Empires used what they called "barbarians" from the eastern steppe region as labor in their mines.[13] As we have seen, slave trading occurred across several regions, not solely along the Ottoman route. Slavic slaves were traded by the Kievan Rus with Germany, some of whom were sold on to Spain.[14] Nevertheless, it was the connection between the Tatars in the Black Sea region and the Ottoman Empire that really consolidated the slave trade in the region.

We have already identified the khanates located within the wider Slavic world as key to the Ottoman slave trade. The most crucial of these was the Crimean Khanate, which was dominated by the Crimean Tatars. The Tatars were people of Turkic origin who had ruled the Crimean Peninsula since the days of the Golden Horde. Tatars had predominantly converted to Sunni Islam and as such, could be allies of the Ottomans. During the high point of the Ottoman Empire, the Crimean Khanate was an outpost of the wider Ottoman territory. Therefore it could act as a gateway to slave traders wanting to sell slaves into the empire. As other European powers increased their influence in the Black Sea region, notably Russia from the seventeenth century onwards, the Ottomans started to lose territory from their peripheral lands, including the Black Sea and Caucasus, which meant the Crimean Khanate became somewhat isolated. Yet, the Grand Duchy of Muscovy—the precursor of Russia—lived in fear of slave raids for centuries. It was not until the rule of Ivan IV, known by history as Ivan the Terrible, that the threat of slave raids began to recede for Russia.[15] Nevertheless, the Crimean Tatars resisted Russian encroachment

---

[11] Citing Duncan Clarke's *Slaves and Slavery* (1998), in: George Pavlu, "Recalling Africa's harrowing tale of its first slavers – The Arabs – as UK Slave Trade Abolition is commemorated," *New African*, 27 March 2018, https://newafricanmagazine.com/16616/, [Accessed 23 June 2021]

[12] Maria Pia Pedani, "Ottoman Merchants in the Adriatic. Trade and Smuggling," Acta Histriae, (16, 2008, 155-172), 162.

[13] Alan Fisher, "Muscovy and the Black Sea Slave Trade", Canadian-American Slavic Studies, (1972, 6:4, 575-594), 576.

[14] Ibid.

for centuries and maintained their place within the Ottoman slave trading network. In its final centuries of independence, the Crimean Khanate acted as somewhat of an affiliated state with Constantinople, while not being an official part of the Ottoman Empire itself.

The tumultuous history of the Crimean Khanate requires a separate book of its own. From its founding in around 1440, the khanate survived against all the odds, constantly threatened by rising Christian powers and sucked into other regional disputes, until 1783 when it was finally absorbed into the Russian Empire ruled by the Romanov Tsars. Key to its longevity was the Tatar's reputation in battle, whose "ferocity" was considered "legendary," according to historian Brian Glyn Williams.[16] This reputation acted as somewhat of a deterrent to nearby powers that wanted to capture the geopolitically important Crimean Peninsula. In fact, for much of this period it was the Crimean Tatars who were on the offensive, launching raids into the surrounding lands to capture and sell Slavs as slaves. The countries surrounding Crimea included Russia to the east, or the Duchy of Moscow as it was known. To the north was today's Ukraine, which at various points was ruled by the Polish-Lithuanian Commonwealth as well the Cossack state, the Hetmanate. Other states also provided targets for the Crimean Tatars, such as Circassia to the east and Hungary to the west. Crucially, the Crimean Tatars sought Christians to sell into the slave trade into the Ottoman Empire.

Christian documents from the medieval period are ambiguous on slavery. Historians have shown how writers from the era abhorred the Crimean Tatar slave trade, one in particular from the early seventeenth century describing the Tatars as "the detestable people of Satan," while at the same time not holding the practices of their own rulers and countries to the same standards.[17] This is perhaps not particularly noteworthy as there were murderous disputes within Christianity let alone between rival faiths such as Christianity and Islam. Nevertheless, it is also interesting that the Crimean Tatars were picked out for special opprobrium from within the Islamic world due to their slave trading practices. Historian Mikhail Kizilov, in his study of Crimea, has outlined how most Christian accounts of the Tatar slave trade were written based on hearsay and distorted by political agendas.[18]

It is estimated that around 2.5 million slaves, most of them Slavs, were brought to the Ottoman Empire through the Crimea and Black Sea route. The method of removing Slavic people from their homes and forcibly selling them into the Ottoman Empire was relatively straightforward. Crimean Tatar raiders, on horseback, would launch surprise assaults on unsuspecting villages in the Slavic areas we have already identified to the north, east and west of Crimea. Civilians would then be kidnapped and forced on slave marches, transiting through the slave port of Caffa, to be

---

[15] Jeremy Black, *A Brief History of Slavery: A New Global History* (Robinson, 2011)
[16] Brian Glyn Williams, *The Sultan's Raiders: The Military Role of the Crimean Tatars in the Ottoman Empire* (Washington DC: Jamestown Foundation, 2013), 40.
[17] Mikhail Kizilov, Slave Trade in the Early Modern Crimea From the Perspective of Christian, Muslim, and Jewish Sources, *Journal of Early Modern History* (2007, 11: 1-2), 12, citing Richard Wendover, published in 1625.
[18] Ibid, 13-14.

sold onwards to Constantinople. Traders would make money on the slaves along the route, details of which will be outlined later. In fact, the raiders would often try to claim ransom immediately, and therefore return those who had been kidnapped to their homes if the money was paid. As a result, many Slavic populations in the regions surrounding the Crimean Khanate and bordering the Ottoman Empire were fearful of raids, building into the dread associated with the Crimean Tatars. In addition, the raiders often struck during times of war, when the soldiers who could have defended the villages were away fighting a campaign. Another tactic employed by the Crimean Tatars was essentially prison, or slave, exchanges. They would imprison Slavs they had captured and attempt to bargain them to return prominent Tatars, including noblemen, who had been captured to Christian powers.[19]

Historians like Alan Fisher have outlined the broad approach of the Crimean Tatars in the slave trade: "Large numbers of slaves-men, women, and children-were brought by the raiding parties to the Crimea (they were called esir, the Turkish word for slave). After negotiations with merchants, often foreign, they were sold and most were shipped to eager buyers abroad. Although some slaves were sold to Europeans, the majority became the chattel of Muslim owners."[20]

Some accounts of Tatar slave raids have described how soldiers would prepare for several weeks before an action. More experienced troops would then go ahead early to the target village and capture an informer for intelligence on the area. The forces would then launch a raid, moving as quickly as possible through a village, avoiding direct confrontation with defenders wherever possible, capturing as many people as they could, and often plundering and razing anything that got in their way.[21]

One of the first major raids by the Crimean Tatars in neighboring lands came in 1468 in Galicia, situated mostly in the west of today's Ukraine. Some estimates of the frequency of the Tatar's slave raids include capturing between 150,000 to 200,000 people in the first half of the seventeenth century, and 38 raids into Slavic lands from 1654 to 1657. Another estimate showed 52,000 people were captured in the spring of 1655 in raids in Ukraine and southern Russia.[22]

The Crimean raids were closely associated with those of the Nogai Horde. The Nogai were another legacy group that survived the end of the Mongol Empire and the Golden Horde. Indeed, the Nogai Khan claimed to be a direct descendent of Genghis Khan. Situated to the east of the Crimean Khanate and bordering the Caspian Sea, the Nogai were also nominally under the authority of the Crimean Khan. Founded in the mid-fifteenth century, the Nogai endured less

---

[19] Gábor Kármán, Lovro Kunčević, *The European Tributary States of the Ottoman Empire in the Sixteenth and Seventeenth Centuries* (Brill, 2013), 292.
[20] Alan Fisher, "Muscovy and the Black Sea Slave Trade", Canadian-American Slavic Studies, (1972, 6:4, 575-594), 575.
[21] Mikhail Kizilov, Slave Trade in the Early Modern Crimea From the Perspective of Christian, Muslim, and Jewish Sources, *Journal of Early Modern History* (2007, 11: 1-2), 8.
[22] Ibid, 6.

time than the Crimean Tatars—finally being absorbed by the Russian Tsar in the 1630s—but nevertheless were synonymous with the raids and slave trading described in this book. As a result, raids during this period, from the mid-fifteenth to mid-seventeenth century, were often called Crimean-Nogai raids.

Although Russia was a rising power during the seventeenth century, it still did not have the clout to really take on the Crimean Tatars. According to historians of the region, the Russian Tsars during this period, "realized very well the Crimean Tatars supported by the Ottoman Empire were too strong both politically and militarily for Muscovy to directly oppose."[23] The slave trade was closely intertwined with Russia's geopolitical position in the region and its rationale for trying to defeat the khanate. The Russian Muscovy state was forced to pay ransom for Russian slaves captured during the Tatar raids, as well as the so-called *pominki,* essentially a tribute from Moscow to the khanate.[24] During the first half of the seventeenth century, this became increasingly difficult for the Russians to pay.[25] With financial constraints, the Russians reasoned that the only way to put an end to the problems posed by the Crimean Tatar slave raids and tribute system was to deter it militarily.

In fact, Russians started to build defensive barriers to keep out the Crimean Tatars during the fifteenth century. During the following century, three defense lines made of fortified towns and obstacles were constructed and manned by locals, as well as Cossacks and local militia.[26] These included the "Abatis Line," built from Ryazan to the Seversk region and then subsequently the "Belgorod Line," which stretched for some 1,000 kilometers.[27] During the seventeenth century, the Russian defenders transitioned more into an offensive posture and gradually moved the lines southwards. This did act as a successful deterrent to Crimean Tatar slave raids, reducing their frequency and success. Russian (and Cossack) forces could intercept the Tatars before they struck a village, or afterwards if they had captives. The final phase of Russia's expansion into the steppe region lasted from the mid-seventeenth century until it completely dominated the area in the 1780s. This final phase, although at various points could not completely eliminate the threat of slave raids, reduced the capacity of the Crimean Tatars to such an extent they could only rarely threaten major population centers.

One of the key issues that drove the slave trade, and shifted the status quo, was its economic ramifications. While the Crimean Tatars almost completely relied on slave raids to function economically, for Muscovite Russia they acted as a significant drag on its development. Parts of the state budget even had to be reserved for paying ransoms for slaves. The threat of Tatar

---

[23] Eizo Matsuki, *The Crimean Tatars and their Russian-Captive Slaves: An Aspect of Muscovite-Crimean Relations in the 16th and 17th Centuries*, 181. http://hermes-ir.lib.hit-u.ac.jp/hermes/ir/re/14906/chichukai0001801710.pdf, [Accessed 20 June 2021]
[24] Ibid.
[25] Ibid.
[26] Ibid.
[27] Jeremy Black, *A Brief History of Slavery: A New Global History* (Robinson, 2011)

attacks and being sold into slavery also caused many Russian peasants to migrate, including a significant number to the cold climate of Siberia, where at least the soil was fertile and threat of political insecurity was reduced.[28]

Nevertheless, the direction of travel during the seventeenth and eighteenth centuries was clearly in favor of Russian expansionary power despite continued slave raids. It is perhaps surprising that the Crimean Tatars and Nogai managed to survive in an increasingly hostile neighborhood as long as they did. Although the Eurasian region more generally was considered the "Wild Fields" of scarcely populated wilderness, it became increasingly dominated by Christian states, notably the Polish-Lithuanian Commonwealth and Russia (and its precursors). Wild Fields was the term given to the steppe region in Polish-Lithuanian texts during that commonwealth's ascendency, between around the sixteenth and eighteenth centuries.[29] It included today's southern and eastern Ukraine, the Crimean Peninsula and some of the surrounding region. Essentially, the Wild Fields were considered an untamed wilderness and are central to our story. Once dominated by the Mongol Empire and the Golden Horde, when that political dominance retreated, a vacuum of power existed. At the crossroads of Europe, Asia and the Middle East, this strategically important region was where other powers sought to assert their influence.

An article by Anne Bobroff-Hajal examined the unique geography of the Steppe region north of the Black Sea, outlining why it was particularly vulnerable to attack.[30] The Steppe region is a flat and exposed region, and this gave raiders from the Crimean Khanate plenty of opportunity to launch short, sharp attacks. Essentially, there was no geography to protect the Slavic populations. Whereas the land was fertile, which had been a prime reason to settle this area in the first place, the lack of a mountain chain provided no natural defense point. From the point of view of the Russian Empire, which even into the eighteenth century was vulnerable to the Tatar slave raids, controlling the steppe became a geopolitical necessity. In the long period of conflict between the Tatars, and the Ottomans more generally, at the south of the steppe region, many Russian conscripts were deployed to serve at the frontier. Because the raids were so regular, often yearly, members of the Russian gentry were even sent to reinforce the area.[31] According to Bobroff-Hajal, "Every member of the Russian gentry was responsible for military duty at the frontier for one half of every summer to protect the expansive southern border against slave raids."[32] This, perhaps, gave Russia's leaders and elite class a unique experience of, and stake in, controlling the region and preventing slave raids. Neutralizing the Crimean Tatar threat would become an

---

[28] Eizo Matsuki, *The Crimean Tatars and their Russian-Captive Slaves: An Aspect of Muscovite-Crimean Relations in the 16th and 17th Centuries*, 181. Ibid.
[29] Gábor Kármán, Lovro Kunčević, *The European Tributary States of the Ottoman Empire in the Sixteenth and Seventeenth Centuries* (Brill, 2013), 127.
[30] Anne Bobroff-Hajal, "Mongol Occupation and the Slav Slave Trade: The 'Harvesting of the Steppe'", Terrain (28, Fall/Winter 2011)
[31] Ibid.
[32] Ibid.

imperative for the Tsarist regime.

Nevertheless, the power vacuum and competition allowed statelets like the Nogai and the Crimean Khanate to survive for centuries. It also meant the absence of authority allowed the raids that kidnapped people and forced Slavs into the slave trade to happen more easily. Often, with the exception of the gradual Russian attempts, there were no effective deterrents or defenses to prevent raiders' incursions. There was another notable exception to this narrative, however, which we will return to later: the rise of the Cossacks.[33]

As a result, the khanate needed to come to agreements with its neighbors via treaties. With their slave raids, the Crimean Tatars and Nogai were often breaking the terms of these treaties. This was less of a problem when the Ottoman Empire was in the ascendency and therefore the fear factor was greater. As the Ottomans went into their long retreat, however, the Nogai, then the Crimean Khanate, became increasingly vulnerable to attack due to their own methods. Russia could, with some justification, claim that by annexing areas of the Ottoman Empire and ultimately Crimea itself, it was protecting Slavic people and the Orthodox Christian faith.

Although the ultimate destination of slaves in the Ottoman Empire was not always draconian—we have already noted that some slaves from the Balkans in particular could reach elevated positions—the route from capture by Tatar raiders to Constantinople was often brutal and sometimes fatal. People kidnapped by the Tatars would be tied together and forced to march to the Crimean Peninsula, often being unable to rest or sleep for days and without food. Captured Slavs would be chained to oars on boats and sometimes were worked to death or died of exhaustion.

However, the Crimean Khanate would not sell every person they captured in raids. Historians have documented how Crimean Tatars rarely cultivated their own land themselves but rather used slaves. As well as working the land, the Tatars would also use slaves as domestic workers and artisans.[34] But those captured would not only be used as labor. The Tatars realized they could use the people they captured as leverage and essentially kept prisoners of war to use as bargaining chips, and this was particularly true of seized Cossacks. Slaves could be used as currency to buy goods such as clothes, horses and weapons.[35] Yet, the trade could even work in the other direction. Struggling families have been described by historians of the region and the slave trade as being willing to essentially sell a child to slave traders in times of hunger or to avoid paying tribute to a ruler.[36]

---

[33] Gábor Kármán, Lovro Kunčević, *The European Tributary States of the Ottoman Empire in the Sixteenth and Seventeenth Centuries* (Brill, 2013), 128.
[34] Mikhail Kizilov, Slave Trade in the Early Modern Crimea From the Perspective of Christian, Muslim, and Jewish Sources, *Journal of Early Modern History* (2007, 11: 1-2), 10.
[35] Ibid, 11.
[36] Ibid.

Caffa was the main port city on the Crimean Peninsula, where captives would be bought at various times by Armenian, Greek, Jewish and Turkish slave traders. Today Caffa is known as Feodosia and is located around 200 kilometers from the Crimean capital, Sevastopol. The slaves would then be transported across the Black Sea to the imperial center, Constantinople and Ottoman government officials would then inspect them upon arrival. After this vetting, typically half of the slaves would be allocated for government use and this was mainly, as we have already seen, through the *devshirme* route from the Balkans, for deployment in administrative and military roles. However, slaves taken by the Crimean Tatars tended to have less prestige and fewer rights than those of the *devshirme* and the janissary class of soldiers. A clear example of the difference between Balkan slaves and those obtained by the Crimean route was how they were used by the military. Whereas *devshirme* would often lead to elevated and even elite positions in the army, Slavic slaves from the Crimean route would frequently be used as oarsmen to power ships. This latter role was one of the most brutal in the army. Oarsmen were chained to the positions and were essentially only in existence, in the eyes of their commanders, to provide power to their ships. Unsurprisingly, oarsmen used in this way often died of exhaustion.

Slave trading could prove a valuable source of income and this was particularly the case for the khanates. For each person captured, the khan would charge a fee or *savğa* as a percentage. This savğa

could be in the region of 10 to 20%. The Crimean khan took one fifth of the income from slaves, while the *kalga* (the khan's successor) and *nureddin* (a heredity administrative position) would keep 10%. In addition, the khan would collect an annual rent, known as the *saliyane*, which was paid from the income of the slave trade in the Crimean Ottoman harbors.[37]

Other important locations in the region's slave trade included Azak and Gözleve while the largest slave market in the khanate was in Karasubazar (today's Belogorsk), close to the Ottoman border.[38] Slaves would be confined to different locations but higher profile captives would be imprisoned in Chufut-Kale. This was a mountainous fortress close to the Crimean Khanate capital of Bahçeseray. In fact, it was not just unknown villagers who were captured by the Crimean Tatars. Some of the better known captives included a Prince of Transylvania, Polish hetmans and Russian ambassadors.[39]

The fate of female slaves along the Crimean route was again different than the Balkan one, and the situation was not the same for men and women. Female slaves would often be sent to the Imperial harem—consisting of wives, servants, and concubines—and some married officials and military officers. However, many women were forced to become sex slaves. Female slaves were

---

[37] Gábor Kármán, Lovro Kunčević, *The European Tributary States of the Ottoman Empire in the Sixteenth and Seventeenth Centuries* (Brill, 2013), 292.
[38] Mikhail Kizilov, Slave Trade in the Early Modern Crimea From the Perspective of Christian, Muslim, and Jewish Sources, *Journal of Early Modern History* (2007, 11: 1-2), 11.
[39] Ibid.

bought and sold in the Ottoman Empire; buyers would "inspect" the women to estimate their "value." The only method to escape this fate in the empire was marriage, which gave women some degree of freedom from servitude. Ottoman slave traders further discriminated depending on a woman's national origin. For instance, Polish slaves fetched a higher price than Russians, representing the kind of prejudice both towards Slavic people and various Slavic nationalities. Nevertheless, slaves were not completely viewed as "private property" with no rights as slave owners had some rudimentary duties to slaves, for instance to feed and clothe them. Slaves could even take their owners to court if they had been mistreated, which seems somewhat of a contradiction in terms, but represents a different view of the practice than other countries. The differences between the transatlantic slave trade, for example, were stark.

As we have already noted, however, slaves were often used for everyday mundane tasks. Female slaves were also used as "wet nurses" for new-born babies and domestic help within homes. Some slaves were used for a fixed period of time, in many cases seven to nine years of service, and could eventually be freed. One element that played its part in leading to slaves' freedom was religion. We have already seen how the *devshirme* and janissary systems forced the conversion of slaves to Islam and how, despite greater levels of religious tolerance compared to many contemporary states and empires, Muslims received preferential status within the Ottoman Empire. Slaves could also buy their freedom, which seems somewhat unlikely given the very nature of their situation, but some historical sources suggest this was a surprisingly common occurrence.

Some interesting details have been noted regarding the names of slaves after they had converted to Islam. As one historian has documented, "Those males who under some circumstance converted to Islam usually received a new Muslim name. Many of these names were typical only of the slaves, such as Salur (linked to the root sal- ('to let go')), Devlet ('good fortune'), derivations from the word gül ('rose'), and other names related to flowers. A patronymic Abd-allah ('slave of the Allah') was usually added to the first name."[40]

Faith was an intractable issue during this period and particularly acute for slaves. Christian states were often less tolerant of different religions than the Ottomans, with law only applying to Christians and non-believers sitting outside the legal norms of society. Converting to another faith was a serious proposition that would cause someone to be ostracized, or worse. In one example from 1675, Cossacks massacred 3,000 Slavic slaves who decided to return to Crimea.[41] The Cossack leader, the *ataman* Ivan Sirko, justified his actions by wanting to prevent the prisoners "multiplying in the Crimea among the infidels and instead of bringing ruin upon our valiant heads and your own eternal damnation without the cross."[42]

---

[40] Ibid, 22.
[41] Ibid, 17.
[42] Mikhail Kizilov, Slave Trade in the Early Modern Crimea From the con of Christian, Muslim, and Jewish Sources, *Journal of Early Modern History* (2007, 11: 1-2), 17, citing D.I.Yavornitskii, Istoriia Zaporozhskikh kozakov, vol. 2 (Kiev, 1990), 388.

As we have seen, the Crimean Khanate was aligned with, although not officially a component of, the Ottoman Empire. While Constantinople could exercise some degree of control, or at least influence, over the Crimean Tatars, the khanate was not beyond freelancing at times. Indeed, historian of the region Brian Williams has described the Tatars almost as "sub-contractors" of the Ottoman Empire, who had a "penchant for plunder"[43] and who joined Constantinople's military campaigns in part as an opportunity to trade slaves. The relationship has been described by some historians as one of a protectorate, and that the Crimean Khanate increasingly relied upon Ottoman protection to prevent a Russian invasion.[44] In fact, the Crimean Khanate ruled over the eastern part of the Crimean Peninsula from 1475. The Sultan wanted geopolitical control of Crimea as a key crossroads in the region but realized the Tatars could be useful allies, and also recognized them as the heirs to Genghis Khan. In 1475, the Ottoman armies seized parts of Crimea governed by the Greeks, as well as colonies established by the Genoese. The Ottomans, reflecting their growing regional influence, governed over the western part of Crimea. Caffa in the khanate was known as "Small Istanbul,"[45] and Tatar slave raids increased dramatically after the Ottoman conquest. Nevertheless, the Crimean Tatars were certainly motivated primarily out of self-interest rather than emotional commitment to the Ottomans and "had few qualms in…attacking and plundering the lands of the infidel" but "avoided costly military engagements that hindered them on pillaging missions."[46] In this respect, the slave trade was the main driver of the khanate's relationship with the Ottomans.

Other studies have developed the relationship between the Crimean Tatars and the Ottomans further, in particular the centrality of the slave trade. Economic ties, notably the trade of Slavic slaves, grew from the mid-fifteenth century until its demise in the eighteenth century. One study, by Boyles, attributes the increase in slave trading through the Black Sea route to the "social and economic realities in Anatolia," located in today's Turkey.[47] This thirst for slaves has been described as a function of the Ottoman Empire's need for new sources of income, including taxes. To service this growth in "bureaucratization," the Sultan urged the Crimean khan "to increase slave raids" while "Anatolia's persistent need for slaves [was] caused by its people's adherence to Islamic principles regarding slavery."[48] Demand for slaves within the Ottoman Empire only fell as it lost territory, mainly to an expansionist Russia. When Russia captured the Crimean Khanate in the eighteenth century, the Ottomans would lose their main supply of slaves.

---

[43] Brian Glyn Williams, *The Sultan's Raiders: The Military Role of the Crimean Tatars in the Ottoman Empire* (Washington DC: Jamestown Foundation, 2013), 42.
[44] Gábor Kármán, Lovro Kunčević, *The European Tributary States of the Ottoman Empire in the Sixteenth and Seventeenth Centuries* (Brill, 2013), 277.
[45] Mikhail Kizilov, Slave Trade in the Early Modern Crimea From the Perspective of Christian, Muslim, and Jewish Sources, *Journal of Early Modern History* (2007, 11: 1-2), 2.
[46] Brian Glyn Williams, *The Sultan's Raiders: The Military Role of the Crimean Tatars in the Ottoman Empire* (Washington DC: Jamestown Foundation, 2013), 7.
[47] Shawn Christian Boyles, "Slavery and the Ottoman-Crimean Khanate Connection", (Oklahoma State University, 2010), 1.
[48] Ibid.

In addition, there were many instances of Crimean Tatar raids into surrounding territories without the consent of the Ottomans. Williams described these "unauthorized" raids as "harvesting of the Steppe," in reference to the Eurasian and Caucasian region.[49] These were not always in accordance with the wider regional policy of the Ottoman Sultan. Constantinople, after all, was not beyond making *Realpolitik* agreements with Christian powers. And while the Crimean Tatars would also fight for other armies if the conditions and wider aims suited them, slave trading was so essential for the khanate's economy, that "harvesting of the Steppe" became integral to its survival. "Plundering neighboring countries was, therefore, one of the easiest ways of keeping the economic situation in the country on the proper level—slaves had always been among the most needed and demanded commodities to be sold both within the country and without."[50] As historian of the region, Mikhail Kizilov, has noted, the Crimean Khanate economy was "not particularly prosperous."[51] As a result, the slave trade became the "cornerstone" of the Crimean Tatar economy.[52] Other historians have described the Crimean economic model as a successful "business activity" in the sixteenth and seventeenth centuries that maintained Tatar society,[53] albeit at the cost of (non-Tatar) human suffering.

When the khanate was finally absorbed into the Russian Empire in 1783, slave trading of Slavic people declined dramatically. A few decades later, the Ottoman Empire itself would give up the practice. Indeed, other historians have gone further to demonstrate the mutual economic interdependence that existed between the Ottomans and the Crimean Tatars, which revolved around the Slavic slave trade through the Black Sea route. More theoretically, Boyles has suggested this was part of a "core-periphery" relationship between the imperial power and its Crimean proxy that could only function with the exploitation of slaves.[54] Boyles noted, "Ultimately the correlations of data between khanate slave raiding and Anatolian economics suggest a very clear but perhaps unintentional relationship of mutual economic interdependency. The more economically powerful partner of the two, the Ottoman Empire, unconsciously affected the power structure and the economic activities, namely slave raiding, of the other due to this interdependence."[55]

As a result, when a faltering Ottoman Empire lost Crimea to Russia in the late eighteenth century, it lost one of its key pillars. It is perhaps no coincidence that the Ottomans went into a steep decline after the loss.

---

[49] Brian Glyn Williams, *The Sultan's Raiders: The Military Role of the Crimean Tatars in the Ottoman Empire* (Washington DC: Jamestown Foundation, 2013).
[50] Mikhail Kizilov, Slave Trade in the Early Modern Crimea From the Perspective of Christian, Muslim, and Jewish Sources, *Journal of Early Modern History* (2007, 11: 1-2), 2.
[51] Ibid.
[52] Ibid.
[53] Dariusz Kolodziejczyk, "Slave hunting and Slave redemption as a business enterprise: The Northern Black Sea region in the sixteenth to seventeenth centuries" *Oriente Moderno*, (25: 86, no. 1 2006), 149-59.
[54] Shawn Christian Boyles, "Slavery and the Ottoman-Crimean Khanate Connection", (Oklahoma State University, 2010), 43.
[55] Ibid.

The Cossacks and Russia

The Cossacks emerged in the aforementioned Wild Fields region from about the fifteenth century, although the exact timeline is disputed. Cossacks were a highly militarized, partially nomadic society that were based around the Dnieper River region in today's Ukraine, to the north of Crimea, where the khanate was based. Interestingly, the Cossacks, similarly to the Crimean Tatars, had some Turkic ethnic origins. However, the Cossacks were also a mix of Russians, Ukrainians, and Belarusians (using today's geography) and followed Orthodox Christianity. Although relatively small in number, the Cossacks exerted a powerful influence on the region and participated in many of its conflicts, often decisively.

The Cossacks started to form a coherent political entity in the form of the Zaporozhian Sich, which grew in clout between the fifteenth and seventeenth centuries. In some respects the Zaporozhian Cossacks grew in opposition to the Crimean Tatars and the two groups partially mimicked each other. Both had a fearsome reputation in battle, both were relatively small groups with outsized influence, and both launched raids into other territories. While the Crimean Tatars were known for capturing slaves, the Cossacks were focused on what can be described as "plunder," that is to say material gain. Unsurprisingly, given the relative similarities between the Cossacks and the Crimean Tatars, the two groups developed a rivalry. As a result, some of the prisoners captured on both sides would be used to secure high profile releases.

The Zaporozhian Sich would be allied to larger powers, for instance the Polish-Lithuanian Commonwealth and later Russia, but crucially, it would be part of an anti-Ottoman bloc, therefore being in direct opposition to the Crimean Tatars and the aims of the khanate. Nevertheless, the Cossacks also tried to carve out their own state, the Hetmanate, between 1649 and 1764, before being absorbed into Russia. The tension between the Christian powers allowed the Crimean Tatars to continually exploit the region and continue the raids that kept the slave trade in business.

Historians have identified a key role to the Cossacks in the weakening of the Ottomans and their Crimean Tatar proxies and ultimately changing the balance of power in the Black Sea: "[The Cossacks] broke the stability of the Black Sea region and threatened the whole concept of the Darü'l-Islam, i.e. the lands governed by the Islamic laws and religion."[56]

As a result, Cossacks were often treated differently to Slavic prisoners if captured. Rather than be sold, Cossacks might be violently executed, presumably in an attempt to deter Cossack raids. Nevertheless, as with so many elements of the geopolitics of the Black Sea region and the wider fault line between Russia, the Ottomans and other European powers, age-old rivalries could be set aside for contingent reasons. For instance, a group of Cossacks led by Ignas Nekrasov in the

---

[56] Mikhail Kizilov, Slave Trade in the Early Modern Crimea From the Perspective of Christian, Muslim, and Jewish Sources, *Journal of Early Modern History* (2007, 11: 1-2), 19.

eighteenth century tried to escape persecution by Russian leader Peter the Great. Nekrasov's Cossacks actually found refuge with the Tatars and even fought on the side of the Crimean Khanate army against the Russians: a case of "my enemy's enemy is my friend."[57]

The relationship between the Cossacks, Russia and the neighborhood changed with the advent of the Cossack Hetmanate in 1649. This development has been seen differently by historians, with some—admittedly more pro-Russian—seeing the Hetmanate as a fraternal joining of Russia, the Cossacks and the wider Ukrainian people. Others, however, have viewed the Hetmanate as the first move towards an independent Ukraine and the distinction matters for our narrative. If the former has more salience, it would likely have reduced the influence of the Ottomans and Tatars as the pro-Russia bloc expanded and sought to limit the Slavic slave trade. The second interpretation presents a more fractured view of the Black Sea region, which the Tatars could continue to exploit with slave raids.

The slave trade looked a secure and permanent part of the wider region even in the seventeenth century. After all, it was not until the following two centuries that the supposedly "enlightened" western countries began to take steps to curb their own slave trade. Yet, we can see the stirrings of uprisings from the slaves themselves. With the other tumult gripping the region in the 1650s, there was an attempt to organize a large-scale insurrection in the Crimea during the decade. Historians have outlined how slaves captured by the Crimean Tatars at the time were "driven to desperation."[58] Nevertheless, the 1650s uprising was discovered at the planning stage and its leaders were punished severely.

Perhaps unsurprisingly, Ottoman and Muslim sources took a different view of the Slavic slave trade. Some of the intricacies of the Ottoman slave trade and the manner in which different faiths were treated in the empire come to the fore. Clearly, Ottoman sources saw the primacy of the Islamic religion as well as the power of the empire itself. As a result, the actions of the Crimean Tatars could be seen as serving a greater good, that of the empire. In addition, the Ottomans could also take a harsher view of the slave raids; that they were the result of the inherent weaknesses and inferiority of Christian countries. There also seemed to be some admiration for the perceived courage and even audacity of the Tatar forces, as fellow Muslims.[59] On the other hand, the Constantinople elites could take a more derisory view of the Crimean Tatars, viewing them as parochial and brutal. Mikhail Kizilov describes the testimony of Muslim author Evliya Çelebi, who "often made contemptuous remarks about the primitiveness and harshness of the Tatar state and people…[and] often felt compassion towards the tortured and humiliated Christians."[60]

We have mainly focused on Muslim slave traders capturing and selling Orthodox Christians

---

[57] Ibid, 20.
[58] Ibid, 15.
[59] Ibid, 24.
[60] Ibid.

into the Ottoman Empire, particularly through Crimea. It should also be noted that many Jewish people were also enslaved along the same route. Some historians have also outlined the role of Jews in Crimea, including facilitating the slave trade itself. Kizilov, for instance, describes how, although many of the historical accounts cannot be trusted, there is evidence that Crimean Jews helped "facilitate" the slave trade on the peninsula.[61] Another historian, Alan Fisher, has written how a guild of Jewish slave merchants, consisting of 2,000 members, existed in Constantinople.[62] More modern historians have viewed the Slavic slave trade, unsurprisingly, as brutal and inhumane, although some have pointed out that fewer critical accounts existed when the slave trade was actually happening. Nevertheless, authors from the Slavic countries themselves have put particular emphasis on the practice. As Kizilov describes, "They could not tolerate the idea of thousands of their co-religionists being constantly belittled and humiliated by the infidel-Muslims and exposed to the 'vicious' influence of Islam."[63]

In retrospect we can see the seventeenth century as the crucial period when Russia began to rise and the Crimean Khanate became fatally weakened. The fall of the Ottoman Empire would come later but it too would be damaged by these events. At the time, however, the Crimean Tatars managed to survive and continued slave raids and trading. Indeed, in some respects the sixteenth century was the zenith of the Black Sea slave trade in Slavs. Why then, can we see a decline in the khanate's situation during this century? The simple answer is the spectacular expansion of Russia under the Romanov dynasty, and the growing power of its Tsars. In essence, the Crimean Khanate became surrounded by Russia and its allies. The Russian Tsar adopted the position as titular leader of both Orthodox Christians and, although more nebulously, the Slavic peoples more generally. As a result, Russia also had in its sights the Slavic slave trade to solidify its role as defender of the Orthodox faith, as well as the fear and moral indignation felt by many towards the practice.

The Crimean Tatars were at war almost constantly between the late 1640s and mid-1660s. As we have seen, wars prevented opportunities for the Tatars to launch slave raids. Nevertheless, this 20-year period brought into being a serious threat to the geopolitical status quo, in so far as it existed. The 1654 Treaty of Pereyaslav between the Cossacks and the Russians provided semi-autonomy to a Cossack state, the Hetmanate, alongside a mutual security guarantee. Russian troops were committed to assisting the Cossacks and vice versa. Others have viewed the treaty as a Cossack pledge of allegiance to Russia, although this has been debated by historians. For the Crimean Khanate, a unification of neighboring forces under Russian leadership presented an existential threat to its continued unique regional role.

The slave trade persisted for the rest of the century because the Crimean Tatar forces still had

---

[61] Ibid, 27.
[62] Alan Fisher, "Muscovy and the Black Sea Slave Trade", Canadian-American Slavic Studies, (1972, 6:4, 575-594), 584.
[63] Mikhail Kizilov, Slave Trade in the Early Modern Crimea From the Perspective of Christian, Muslim, and Jewish Sources, *Journal of Early Modern History* (2007, 11: 1-2), 29.

enough military prowess and numbers, and because Russia was not quite strong enough to land a decisive blow against the khanate or the Ottomans. In addition, and perhaps counterintuitively, some of the Western European powers were willing to prop up Constantinople due to concerns over an expansionist Russia. Nevertheless, the 1699 Treaty of Karlowitz was Russia's attempts to end the Tatar raids into its territory. The treaty forced the khanate to accept that raids into Russian territory would be considered illegal and therefore necessitate a military response from the Romanovs.[64]

By maintaining autonomy, the Crimean Khanate was able to continue slave raids and trading into the eighteenth century. The Ottoman Empire was still one of the world's major powers and, as we have seen, the supply of Slavic slaves from the Black Sea region powered the Ottoman's economic and societal model. Nevertheless, the new arrangement between Russia and the khanate after 1699 constrained the Crimean Tatars. The capture of Slavs from the surrounding region continued to affect relations between the two states and despite the treaty, the Tatars continued to launch slave raids, including into Russia.[65] This was an affront to the Russian authorities and induced insecurity into the local Slavic populations. Yet, it also provided the *casus belli* for the Tsarist regime to attack the Tatars and inflict a perhaps ultimate defeat on the khanate. After all, the statelet broke the terms of the 1699 treaty on numerous occasions during the following century and it was never likely to be otherwise. As we have already discussed, the Crimean Khanate economy relied on the slave trade for hard currency and its symbiotic relationship with the Ottoman Empire also needed the supply of labor. Despite the treaty with Russia, the khanate saw few alternatives to its forays into the surrounding region and to perpetuate the slave trade.

During one the Crimean Tatars last raids into Slavic territory in 1769, into Poland and Russia, 20,000 people were captured.[66] Tatar raids, however, diminished during the eighteenth century due to the growing strength of Russia in the region.[67] As the eighteenth century progressed, Ottoman power went into relative decline compared to other European states. Russia expanded rapidly and it was now considered an empire, covering an ever greater landmass, and including more and more people. Russia and the Ottomans fought several wars, not only over contested areas such as the Caucasus, but also for territory held by the Sultan and coveted by the Tsar. In a conflict during the 1730s, the Russian army made a crucial breakthrough and gained a foothold on the Crimean Peninsula. Russian military commanders laid waste to the Crimean cities they captured, decimating much of the khanate. The 1739 Treaty of Niš, negotiated between the Russians (led by Catherine the Great) and the Ottomans, saw the former's withdrawal from most of Crimea but permitted Russia to build a port at Azov on the Black Sea. This gave the Russians

---

[64] Abou-el-Haj A. Rifaat, "The Formal Closure of the Ottoman Frontier in Europe: 1699-1703," *Journal of the American Oriental Society*, 89:3 (1969): 467-75.

[65] Mikhail Kizilov, "Slave Trade in the Early Modern Crimea From the Perspective of Christian, Muslim, and Jewish Sources", *Journal of Early Modern History* (2:1-2, 2007, 1-31)

[66] Ibid, 7.

[67] Ibid, 6.

crucial access to the region's major waterway and through which the slave trade passed towards Constantinople. Catherine would also renounce Russia's claim on Crimea, although that pledge was discarded a few decades later.

The Crimean Tatars may have been geographically boxed in after the 1699 and 1739 treaties, but they managed to continue to capture Slavic slaves, often at a high frequency. In fact, some of the biggest slave raids of the entire Crimean Khanate period occurred as the statelet itself stood on the brink of being invaded by Russia. Ultimately, the war that snuffed out Crimean Tatar autonomy and reoriented the peninsula from the Ottoman sphere of influence to the Russian one took place between 1768 and 1774. As became a pattern in the Black Sea region, it was fought between multiple protagonists, across south-eastern Europe and beyond. Other Christian states, for instance the Greeks, joined the common cause against the Ottoman and khanate forces. Russia and its allies triumphed in the conflict and, in the 1774 peace treaty, compelled the Ottoman Sultan to accept that the Crimean Khanate was independent from Constantinople. This did not mean immediate Russian annexation, but paved the way for Tsarist coercion of the Tatars.[68] After the many wars of the eighteenth century, Russia now controlled Crimea and a strategic position on the Black Sea. With it, Russia could now virtually put an end to the Slavic slave trade.

Russia, under the Tsarina Catherine the Great, formally annexed the Crimean Khanate in December 1783. The seizure occurred after several years of Tatar revolts against Russian interference on the peninsula. The Russian military used the pretext of quelling the uprisings as the justification for annexation. Crucially, Russia, as the designated protector of Orthodox Christians, partly justified the move by saying it wanted to protect Christians living on the peninsula. After years of war and growing Russian pressure, the Crimean Tatars were militarily exhausted, and out of allies and resources. The khanate was incorporated into the Russian Empire as the Taurida Oblast and as Kizilov remarked, the worst was over for Slavic populations living in fear of Tatar raids. "It was only in 1774-1783 that the Russian annexation of the peninsula stopped for good this inhuman trade of live objects."[69]

The Decline of the Slave Trade in Eastern Europe

As we have seen, Russia's capture of the Crimean Khanate was not solely geopolitical. The Tsarist regime could present itself as protector of both Slavs and the Orthodox faith, despite the widespread penury and persecution that still existed within its own borders. Indeed, the system of "serfdom" (essentially agricultural slavery for peasants) persisted in Russia until it was abolished in the 1860s. This is not an inconsequential point. When serfdom was abolished in Russia in 1861, it is estimated around half the Russian population was in fact a serf.[70] As well as

---

[68] Henri Troyat, *Catherine the Great* (Plume, 1994)
[69] Mikhail Kizilov, Slave Trade in the Early Modern Crimea From the Perspective of Christian, Muslim, and Jewish Sources, *Journal of Early Modern History* (2007, 11: 1-2), 31.
[70] Andrei Konchalovsky, "The living legacy of Russia's slavery," Open Democracy, 9 September 2011,

agricultural serfs, household serfs were also very common. As one historian puts it, "Slavery in Russia was an important institution."[71] It is against this backdrop that we must posit the Slavic slave trade with the Islamic world. Slavery was completely normalized in Russia and despite being the appointed protector of Orthodox Christians and Slavs, the Russian elites had seemingly little problem in enslaving their brethren. It was only slowly that this situation changed. Attitudes did shift gradually in Russia and in what Europeans know as the "Enlightenment" (during the eighteenth and nineteenth centuries), Russian society and its intelligentsia were seemingly locked in a debate over whether the country should be more orientated towards Europe or to a more idiosyncratic, partly east-facing, particular Russian path. As a result, some progressive and liberal thinking percolated into elite discourse, including over the appropriateness and ethics of slavery. At the same time, Russian nationalism grew, which meant the capture of Russians by an outside power would have been viewed as increasingly intolerable.

Nevertheless, security under Russian protection against the threat of Tatar slave raids and being sold into the Ottoman Empire to be converted to Islam would have had an emotional resonance for many. Russia used its version of "soft power" to support other Slavic and Orthodox states break from larger empires, notably from the Ottomans, during the nineteenth century. Russia would support and in some cases provide security guarantees to the new states of Greece, Bulgaria, Serbia and Montenegro. The biggest exception to this was the Crimean War of 1853-1856 when western European powers Britain and France supported the Ottoman Empire in its war against Russia for control of the peninsula. This was, however, pure geopolitics. The Ottomans were trying to reclaim some of their lost territory while Britain and France were concerned about the growing strategic influence and power of Russia. For its part, Russia wanted to consolidate its gains and access to the Black Sea was crucial. The conflict was inconclusive. Ostensibly the anti-Russian coalition triumphed but within a few years Russia had reasserted itself on the peninsula and continued to rise within European politics. The Crimean War gave hope to the Crimean Tatars that the pre-1783 status quo might be restored. Following the war, the Russian authorities blamed Tatars for collaborating with the Ottoman side and made life more difficult for many people on the peninsula. As a result, around 200,000 Crimean Tatars fled their homes and emigrated to the Ottoman Empire.[72]

In summary, the nineteenth century saw a continued growth in Russian territory and power while Ottoman influence declined. The slave trade, too, was in steep decline. By the time the Crimean Tatars were in the minority on the lands of the former khanate, the Black Sea slave trade was over. Yet, it continued elsewhere at the same time as a burgeoning global movement to abolish slavery.

---

https://www.opendemocracy.net/en/odr/living-legacy-of-russias-slavery/, [Accessed 24 June 2021]
[71] Ibid.
[72] Johannes Remy, "Russia and Crimea: Heroism and ethnic cleansing," *Baltic Rim Economies* (2019), https://sites.utu.fi/bre/russia-and-crimea-heroism-and-ethnic-cleansing/

Western European countries had come under pressure to abolish their involvement in the slave trade during the eighteenth century. Indeed, the British and French empires had grown rich from the transatlantic slave route that was arguably more draconian than slavery in the Ottoman Empire. The British government effectively banned slavery in 1807 and France, albeit more spasmodically, also took steps to outlaw the practice around the same time. Having been two of the leading profiteers from slavery for centuries, Britain and France then became abolitionists during the nineteenth century, attempting to ban the slave trade worldwide. The Ottoman Empire would then come under some pressure to curtail its own slave trade. Russia's Tsarist regime also sought to abolish slavery with a focus on the Ottomans. For instance, Russian anti-slavery abolitionists pursued a campaign in the Caucasus to put an end to the practice.[73]

Slavery continued in the Ottoman lands at this time. For instance, many Greeks were enslaved after rising up against Ottoman rule in 1821. However, by the early to mid-nineteenth century the Ottoman Empire was becoming somewhat more progressive and its leadership did act to reduce slavery. In a move that may have been calculated to appease European powers, including Russia, the Ottoman authorities initially limited slavery of white people and then, from 1830, started to grant all white slaves their freedom. Subsequently, the Ottomans further limited slavery of all ethnicities. Part of the pressure on the Ottoman rulers came from an international campaign against what became dubbed "White Slavery" in the first half of the nineteenth century. However, this was mainly focused on slavery into the Ottoman Empire via the Mediterranean and North Africa, as briefly discussed earlier. The "Barbary slave trade" demonstrated that slavery was still present in the Ottoman Empire in the nineteenth century despite the Slavic route's curtailment due to Russia's annexation of Crimea. Western European countries, as well as the United States, actually fought two wars, in 1801-1805 and 1815, to stop the Barbary route, although typically this culminated in European countries expanding their own empires into North Africa, for instance, in today's Algeria and Tunisia.

The Ottomans came under most pressure from Western countries over slavery just as Britain and France banned their own participation in the trade. Perhaps surprisingly, discussions about the ethics of slavery permeated into Ottoman society itself. Historian Ehud R. Toledano has written that "the call for the abolition of Ottoman slavery was perhaps the most culturally loaded and sensitive topic processed in the *Tanzimat* period."[74] The *Tanzimat* era lasted from around the mid-1830s until the mid-1870s in the empire, during the reigns of Sultans Abdülmecid I and Abdülaziz. The Ottoman Empire, in hindsight, was moving into its final phase and its leaders sought to maintain its power and prestige. Perhaps surprisingly, the direction it took during the *Tanzimat* was to introduce a number of European-facing reforms. For instance, the Sultans sought to implement basic rights more in keeping with a nineteenth century state than the historic Ottoman regime aligned more clearly with theocracy. In addition, the *Tanzimat* sought to provide

---

[73] L. Kurtynova-D'Herlugnan, *The Tsar's Abolitionists: The Slave Trade in the Caucasus and Its Suppression*, (Leiden: Brill, 2010)

[74] Ehud R. Toledano, "Late Ottoman Concepts of Slavery (1830s-1880s)," *Poetics Today*, 14(3), 1993, 477-506.

more equality between Muslims and the empire's other faiths. Education became more secular and conscription in the military was introduced. In this environment, it was unsurprising that the institution of slavery came under strain.

Attempts by Ottoman rulers during the nineteenth century to curtail slavery may have worked in practice, but legally it remained an area of uncertainty. During the *Tanzimat* period, Ottoman reformers sought to sweep away the old religiously-based legal and court system (the *Seriat*) to introduce a more secular model. However, even by the end of the *Tanzimat*, slavery remained uncodified on the new statutes and therefore still fell within the scope of the old *Seriat*.[75] Interference from France, and in particular Britain, during the nineteenth century became more acute due to the encroachment of Western empires in North Africa and the Middle East. Britain's role in Egypt is particularly pertinent here. Hakan Erdem has written how a schism developed within British decision-making circles between those who proposed trying to suppress the practice, and others who sought to abolish it. Certainly, Britain could exert some pressure on the Ottomans by claiming a kind of moral "high ground" having recently ended slavery, despite its own involvement prior to that for centuries.[76]

One of the more unique elements about slavery in the Ottoman Empire was how the structures put in place by the idiosyncrasies of the practice led to challenges to the Sultan and his coterie in implementing reform. The obvious example was the janissary class. We have already noted how children and teenagers—not necessarily Slavs but usually Christian—were forcibly taken from families in the Balkan region, converted to Islam and allocated to the janissary regiments, of elite troops. Over centuries the janissaries morphed into a discreet interest group in Ottoman society, perhaps surprisingly as advocates of continuing its institution and as defenders of the status quo. Janissary-led revolts had recurred in Ottoman history—after all, they were elite troops and had independent access to weapons—but occurred with more frequency in the eighteenth century. An uprising in 1730 forced the Sultan to abdicate. Janissaries altered the balance of power in Ottoman-ruled Serbia in 1804, ultimately seeing Belgrade break away from the empire. Further coup attempts happened in 1807-1808 as more modernizing and liberal Sultans sought to Europeanize the empire. The janissaries, on the other hand, were traditionalists and conservatives who opposed reform and wanted to prevent European influence in the empire. Ultimately, the authorities imposed their will on the discontents, with Sultan Mahmud II abolishing the janissary class in 1826 and instituting a modern military. He launched a brutal crackdown against the janissaries and many were executed. The rise and fall of the janissaries was a particular component of history in the Ottoman Empire. The institution of the janissaries was a cunning method of using slaves while maintaining control in the wider empire. It offered slaves the chance for advancement far exceeding other systems in the world at that time. But the slaves themselves then formed a vested interest, which conversely sought to perpetuate the system, to block reform and continue to permit the capture of Christian children as new recruits.

---

[75] Y Hakan Erdem, *Slavery in the Ottoman Empire and its Demise, 1800-1909* (Palgrave Macmillan, 1996)
[76] Ibid.

Despite the janissary uprisings and ultimate defeat, reform in the empire continued. Toledano highlights how, while the process of obtaining slaves was often not a focus of Ottoman discussions, the challenge to the practice shook elite structures in the empire. This is because Western European empires like Britain and France would use slave labor in the most egregious manner, as workers on plantations or other labor-intensive roles. These countries were making clear economic gains by exploiting slaves, then selling or exporting a resource or product. We have already seen how slaves were used differently within the Ottoman Empire, for instance in elite military units. Many slaves, however, were used in domestic settings and were the backbone of how many elite Ottoman families operated. Indeed, the Ottomans wanted to portray their own use of slaves as mainly focused in the domestic sphere—although they did indeed deploy slave labor in agriculture—rather than, for instance, the separate British model. Toledano continues, "British abolitionism must have touched the very core of Ottoman elite culture, where the belief and value systems were most vulnerable to criticism."[77] A few separate points can be made here. First, the Western focus of abolition campaigns was on slavery for economic gain, rather than domestic slavery. When the Ottomans came under pressure to end slavery, however, it was often in the domestic sphere where the practice was most entrenched. In the West, unpaid work in the domestic and agricultural sectors continued long after slavery had been abolished but never received the same attention. Second, the intercultural exchanges between Western Europe and Ottomans during this period reflected the ascent of the former against the decline of the latter. The Ottomans came under pressure to end their own forms of slavery as they came under pressure in many other spheres, including geopolitics.

In 1890, the major powers met in Brussels in Belgium, signing the Brussels Conference Act that suppressed the slave trade. Europe's major leaders attended the 1890 conference, which had followed decades of what became dubbed the "Scramble for Africa," whereby European empires attempted to carve up the continent into colonies. As a result, the focus of the meeting was on Black slavery and although the Ottomans agreed to the communique, the Slavic slave trade was not a major theme. It would not be until the founding of the League of Nations in 1919, the first major international organization, that the scope of trying to ban slavery was widened. In 1926, the Convention to Suppress the Slave Trade and Slavery was agreed under the auspices of the League. By this point, the Ottoman Empire no longer existed but its successor, Turkey, did sign the treaty. Other countries also passed laws to ban "White slavery"; for instance, the US in 1910 with its White-Slave Traffic Act.

Although slavery as a practice continued during the twentieth century and even into our current era, the Slavic slave trade studied in this book had long since disappeared. The rise of Russia threatened the trade and with Catherine the Great's annexation of the Crimean Peninsula at the end of the eighteenth century, the main source of slaves—the Crimean Khanate and its raids into neighboring lands—dried up due to Russian military dominance of the northern Black Sea

---

[77] Ehud R. Toledano, "Late Ottoman Concepts of Slavery (1830s-1880s)," *Poetics Today*, 14(3), 1993, 477-506.

region. The Ottoman Empire itself, which was the destination of the Slavic slaves, also took more progressive steps in the following century, essentially outlawing the practice. Ottoman power also waned during this time while others—notably Russia but also Prussia and its successor Germany—grew in influence. At successive great power conferences and as a result of repeated conflicts, the Ottomans lost territory in the Mediterranean, the Balkans and South East Europe. At the turn of the twentieth century the Ottoman Empire came under renewed pressure from various nationalist groups, including by Turkish nationalists, known as the "Young Turks." Secular and to some extent European-facing, the Young Turks opposed slavery. It would be the First World War, however, that finally finished off the Ottoman Empire, fighting on the losing side along with the "Central Powers" of Germany and Austria against the "Entente Powers" of Russia, Britain, France and the United States. Out of the ashes of the empire came the Turkish Republic, dominated by the Young Turks and most prominent of this new generation of Turkish leaders was Mustafa Kemal Atatürk, the country's first president. Atatürk banned "legal slavery" in Turkey, although he waited until 1933 to ratify the League of Nations' Convention to Suppress the Slave Trade and Slavery.

The Slavic slave trade went into terminal decline at the end of the eighteenth century with Russia's annexation of the Crimean Peninsula. Slavery within the Ottoman Empire itself also fell during the nineteenth century as its leaders felt compelled to try and implement reform. It is important to note that slavery was, although restricted, not abolished even at the end of the Ottoman Empire.[78] This process was not complete until the very end of the empire itself and the emergence of Turkey as a successor state. The memories of the experience of slavery and the slave trade have been relatively repressed in these successor states of the Ottoman Empire. This is partly to their authoritarian nature and partly due to continued nationalism. The legacy of slavery within the Ottoman Empire, including of Slavic slaves, has an unacknowledged legacy in modern-day Turkey. Historians such as Murray Gordon have described this as a "conspiracy of silence."[79] On the Slavic side there has, perhaps unsurprisingly, been more work on the topic. Nevertheless, as we have seen, there is a burgeoning body of historiography on the subject that can provide a relatively full picture of the Slavic slave trade with the Ottoman Empire. Ultimately, however, although much of this story was intertwined with geopolitics and broad patterns of behavior over centuries, its results meant several million people were enslaved and sold like a commodity. Unfortunately, Slavic slavery is one of history's crimes that has received too little attention.

Online Resources

Other books about Islamic history by Charles River Editors

---

[78] Y Hakan Erdem, *Slavery in the Ottoman Empire and its Demise, 1800-1909* (Palgrave Macmillan, 1996)
[79] Ibid.

Further Reading

Jeremy Black, *A Brief History of Slavery: A New Global History* (Robinson, 2011)

Shawn Christian Boyles, "Slavery and the Ottoman-Crimean Khanate Connection", (Oklahoma State University, 2010)

Bayarsaikhan Dashdondog (2019). The Black Sea Slave Trade in the 13th–14th century That Changed the Political Balance in the Near East. *Golden Horde Review*. 7. 283-294.

Y Hakan Erdem, *Slavery in the Ottoman Empire and its Demise, 1800-1909* (Palgrave Macmillan, 1996)

Alan Fisher, *The Crimean Tatars* (Hoover Institution Press, 1978)

Marek Jankowiak, Dirhams for slaves: Investigating the Slavic slave trade in the tenth century, Medievalists (2012) https://www.medievalists.net/2016/02/dirhams-for-slaves-investigating-the-slavic-slave-trade-in-the-tenth-century/, [Accessed 17 June 2021]

Gábor Kármán, Lovro Kunčević, *The European Tributary States of the Ottoman Empire in the Sixteenth and Seventeenth Centuries* (Brill, 2013)

Mikhail Kizilov, "Slave Trade in the Early Modern Crimea From the Perspective of Christian, Muslim, and Jewish Sources", *Journal of Early Modern History* (2:1-2, 2007, 1-31)

Dariusz Kolodziejczyk, "Slave hunting and Slave redemption as a business enterprise: The Northern Black Sea region in the sixteenth to seventeenth centuries" *Oriente Moderno*, (25: 86, no. 1, 2006)

Andrei Konchalovsky, "The living legacy of Russia's slavery," Open Democracy, 9 September 2011, https://www.opendemocracy.net/en/odr/living-legacy-of-russias-slavery/

L. Kurtynova-D'Herlugnan, *The Tsar's Abolitionists: The Slave Trade in the Caucasus and Its Suppression*, (Leiden: Brill, 2010)

Anh Nga Longva, "From the Dhimma to the capitulations: memory and experience of protection in Lebanon," *Religious Minorities in the Middle East: Domination, Self-Empowerment, Accommodation* (Brill, 2012)

Johan MacKechnie, "Justifying Slavery", *History Today* (67:5, May 2017), https://www.historytoday.com/justifying-slavery

Eizo Matsuki, *The Crimean Tatars and their Russian-Captive Slaves: An Aspect of Muscovite-Crimean Relations in the 16th and 17th Centuries*, 181. http://hermes-ir.lib.hit-u.ac.jp/hermes/ir/re/14906/chichukai0001801710.pdf

James E. Montgomery, Ibn Faḍlān and the Rusiyyah, *Journal of Arabic and Islamic Studies*, 3, (2000) 1–25

George Pavlu, "Recalling Africa's harrowing tale of its first slavers – The Arabs – as UK Slave Trade Abolition is commemorated," *New African*, 27 March 2018, https://newafricanmagazine.com/16616/

Maria Pia Pedani, "Ottoman Merchants in the Adriatic. Trade and Smuggling," Acta Histriae, (16, 2008, 155-172)

Johannes Remy, "Russia and Crimea: Heroism and ethnic cleansing," *Baltic Rim Economies* (2019), https://sites.utu.fi/bre/russia-and-crimea-heroism-and-ethnic-cleansing/

Abou-el-Haj A. Rifaat, "The Formal Closure of the Ottoman Frontier in Europe: 1699-1703," *Journal of the American Oriental Society*, 89:3 (1969): 467-75.

Ehud R. Toledano, "Late Ottoman Concepts of Slavery (1830s-1880s)," *Poetics Today*, 14(3), 1993, 477-506.

Henri Troyat, *Catherine the Great* (Plume, 1994)

Brian Glyn Williams, *The Sultan's Raiders: The Military Role of the Crimean Tatars in the Ottoman Empire* (Washington DC: Jamestown Foundation, 2013)

Brian Glyn Williams, *The Crimean Tatars: From Soviet Genocide to Putin's Conquest* (Oxford University Press, 2015)

D.I.Yavornitskii, "Istoriia Zaporozhskikh kozakov", vol. 2 (Kiev, 1990)

Free Books by Charles River Editors

We have brand new titles available for free most days of the week. To see which of our titles are currently free, click on this link.

Discounted Books by Charles River Editors

We have titles at a discount price of just 99 cents everyday. To see which of our titles are currently 99 cents, click on this link.

Printed in Poland
by Amazon Fulfillment
Poland Sp. z o.o., Wrocław

29061130R00020